COLLECTION OF POEMS

Vanessa Ngam

A publication of

Eber & Wein Publishing

Pennsylvania

Collection of Poems

Library of Congress
Cataloging in Publication Data

ISBN 978-1-60880-547-1

Proudly manufactured in the United States of America by

Eber & Wein Publishing

Pennsylvania

Collection of Poems

1

I sniff my nose inside the drapes like a cat

Nauseated from the familiar odor

I turn my back towards the wall

And my face, too

She probably thinks I am drowned

Because of the pills

I feel the presses

Hear the sighs, the groans, too

The space in the middle

Like the wall that separates two

Cities together, such a strong barrier

I am stuck prone facing the rear

The unbroken barrier I am tempted to

Close with a pillow

My open left eye is alert of emergency shifts

Everlasting wall of love that stiffens and widens every day

Leave the Grass Tall

Leave the grass tall—untrimmed, au naturel—
Not at the advantage of angry mowers
Cutting it till you can see the soil.
The lady next door sleeps in earplugs.
The night worker next to me sleeps in mufflers.
The lighter air transmits that sound like
Blowing wind bringing particles to the shore—
Particles and transmission normally lost
In air during the heavy cold, freezing winter.

Sin

Sin, a nightmare, scary

Three-letter word

Buried in deceitful lies

And scornful hate

A scene of guild encapsulates

Humanity from head to toe

Body and spirit protecting

It from being cleansed

A sinful scene grows

In the mind, shifting the good from bad

The ugly from the beautiful and

Difficult to separate in humanity

My Gentle One

My gentle one
Speak softly in that harsh voice
In that light blue wear amidst this heinous heat
Move slowly, speak to him slowly
Tone down the loudness
Tone done the yellow-blue stain
Staining your lips, for it scares
Me like a nightmare

Walk like a gentle model in the street
With a strict-yet-liberal countenance
Evoking an endless stare from passersby
Quirking birds, noisy vehicles, moving trains
Growing silent and drowsy at your footsteps
Regains strength when its foot steps are gone

A Broken Cave

A broken cave

Disjointed, shattered, and crooked

Roofs, dusty ground, old footsteps

Of armed soldiers, large printed fingers

Pinned to the great walls

Vacant of fresh, stale

Pleasant odor

Once homage for our men

Residence for those beaten by the heavy rain

The snowstorm melting on its round roof

Dripping thick liquids like paint

Door endlessly ajar, yet we sleep in

An Empty Room

An empty room
A vacant room for rent
An evacuated room
All items swept by the merciless storm

She stood in there
A sole survivor of the bitter experience
Like a solid rock left in the middle of the ocean
Unable to recollect memories
And the silent wind blew across shoulder pads
And feet and fell to the ground breathless
An endless storm

My Tears Are Solid Salt Pieces

My tears are solid salt pieces
They drop down my face like snowflakes
Morning, day, and night my pillow piles
With sweat and tears

I never knew of tears
My cheeks burst with laughter at your side
Next to me is an empty spot
My strength is gone, I am drowned in tears
Like an overflowing river ready to empty its contents on land
I empty mine on your spot

In Your Image

I saw your face

The smile that never ceases

The voice that sang at our knot ceremony

An everlasting image

Earthquakes and violent thunderstorms are just slow waves

Upright your image stands

Just as we stood still in the ocean

When the strong waves blew us to a clear path

Death is monstrous

Monstrous death am I, stuck with a frame

A frame whose deeds are intact

I smile at you when I wake up

Hello, good morning, and scream in my frustration

Weep from silence

Silence brought forth

By the power of the monster

From Thee Unto Thee

We were made from you and will be you someday.

A great substance the rain pours on thee;

The wind carries thee away to its destination,

Yet your substance still remains.

Children, adults, and all tread on thee—

This great substance.

When I bid farewell to this world,

You will be my port of entry to my resting place.

I am so glad I'll be well protected.

Thy weight will be borne forever.

Man will forever be secured knowing you are

His withstanding path that will forever exist.

A Dreadful Moment

A dreadful moment like a pistol in a cave
Which wrinkled hands and feet and bras fail to support
When voices lost their tone audibility and one gets murmured
And strained ears to hear and wide eyes to see

A moment when the cane guides us to homes
Markets, hospitals, even to make the toilet pot visible
Ears get blocked with aids and teeth with claws for mastication
When one passes gas unconsciously and voids regularly

When young ones point fingers and
Gaze in dismay at wrinkled hands and face
The time the clock is still
Seems like forever will be the same
And tomorrow dreadful

And yesterday as a genius and fresh
And when beat skips
When mouth fails to move
The calling bird fails to respond
When the sky looks white
And the brain like a vast room
Then the time is near

I Remain Strong

I remain strong in the face of tornadoes and earthquakes

Against the bitter winter cold

Against the harsh harmattan

Against the gentle wind

I resist the force of a thousand men trying to let me down

Or destroy me

I am unmoved by the giant hammer

Crackless am I

Intact as the strongest rock I remain

If you hit me you get hit

I am peaceful

I am a rock

HIV-AIDS

It came gradually, started in the eighties.

It came from one person and now is across the globe.

What did man do to deserve your hammer?

You clear intelligent people, gifted persons,

The talented, the reckless, and all.

On none is your mercy shown.

Tell me why you are doing this even to the premature,

The innocent, and the upright.

I have no cousins; you took them all away from me.

Did they deserve your wrath?

All tears from their beds, prayers

Could not soften your soft spot.

Do you even have a soft spot?

Mystery, you know no mercy, no pity for fornicators and rapists,

For the adulterous and the careless,

Not even for the unborn and the tender.

The priests, the reverend sisters, and the chaste—

Do they deserve this, too?

A Beginning Poet

When the evening is calm

And the air still

The cold and freshness from outside

Penetrates through my windows

It's 3:00 a.m. and my eyes stare at corners

I probably had too much of that sweet

Moscato with friends

I need to void and get back to bed

My little room brightens with the light

As I attempt to switch it off again

The printed paper on the wall near

The window draws me near

It's been like that for six months

Still waiting and hoping

For one thrice its size

That which can be framed

Is why I can smile

(My efforts are not in vain)

As I pick up my pen and paper

To write again

Writer's Prayer

Lord, as I commence this path
Guide me in the dark
Provide a long stick to hold onto
To lead my feet to the end
To lead my brain till the end
To take rejections as a challenge
Honorable mentions as hope
And winning as victory
Stumbling blocks, huddles on my path
In a pothole I shall dwell like a
Stockpile of rejection scripts
Shattered and shredded to pieces
And forgotten long, long ago
Let my mind blossom with fresh ideas
Fresh verses leaking on pages
And loading that stockpile

Why I Hate Swimming in the Lake

Because all lakes are water

Because nature's call sometimes occurs in the pool

Because of the color of the water

Because of what they put inside

Because the lake is for everyone

Because sometimes I consume fish from the lake

Because Eric was murdered and dumped in a lake

Because they never beheld his body

Because of atheists and mermaids

So I hate anything white

That looks pure, stainless

But when worn and torn

Looks like a mermaid

About to devour the soul

Life

Life is a roller coaster going up and down
With peaks and falls and occasional bumps
What reason is an elevator in every building
Except that the handicapped need easy access
Though our feet hurt continuously from
Walking and climbing, wishing helplessly
For cars to walk the paths for us
Mankind likes easy-to-go life
I bump into neighbors' cats
And dogs that scare me
Climbing the stairs is tedious but worth the pain

A Father's Advice to a Daughter

My daughter, do not blunder;

take time and get a reliable partner.

Two feet can never be the same

though for same aim.

Treat all with respect

for all deserve respect.

Avoid endless blame.

Strive to remain sane and tame.

Continue to be focused and never be furious.

Find someone who is serious.

Nev'r be with one 'cause of fame

for that will one day drive you insane.

Find someone to be with forever.

A misname give us never.

I Shall Continue to Strive

I shall continue to strive

Though all seems dark and bleak

For it does not hurt to fight when all seems to leak

I shall continue to strive

For at the end of the tunnel is a light

That shines and reflects in a stream

We shall continue to try

Our tears are our flight

That with, speak

I shall continue to try

I know little smile but might

Shall soon be my reach

I shall continue to strive

For victory will be my pride

And misfortunes wreak

I shall continue to strive

We shall continue to try

The Necklace

The necklace given to you
By your late mum, I found
It in the dustbin. You had said I stole
It from your neck to sell it for latest trends.
You forget I am a student as you.
Its rare stones were intact. What caught my
Attention were such stones amidst rocks, dust, and
Graded papers. You scored A's in all.
Something believed to be an aftermath of that
Precious thing. You told me your hope and
Hustle grew fresh as leaves in early spring at its site.
It was removed and dumped by someone.
Your conscience knows
I was strangled by your soft hands
And vibrated as your little and soft voice
United our enemies and friends.
You smile now as the piece hangs glowing
From your neck. You had your way again.

Yesterday

Yesterday I was hot-tempered

Yesterday I was a thief

I stole your words

Your words of wisdom

My students say

We know that phrase

We know it from somewhere

I am not ashamed to tell them

Y'all are right. That is my co-teacher word

Today All Awaited the Snow

The streets are still and quiet as a graveyard

The tornado has come and passed

The busy street is empty and the only sound is the train

And the smoke from its roof

Everyone is home

Those at work cling there

It is supposed to be five inches

Even rumored to deprive roofs and flood houses

Our hearts are not with us

Our brains have been stolen

The moment is still and the clock timeless

Outside is blurred, dark, cold, breezy, and windy

Thunderstorms fighting each other

It starts raining and the evening gets darker

We get to bed with our hearts stolen away from us

By fear of nature and its elements

Mixed Feelings

When fantasies and nightmares crowd the mind

Like flies chasing feces

The desire to be released

From bondage and darkness to light and paradise

The desire to meet foreign people, tongue twists words and

Gives a false smile

The final day is welcomed like one envisages

To be greeted in paradise

The moment in the boarding line

Brings tears to the eyes and uneasiness

The final wave of goodbye to the ones

Who always cared is like the final wave of glory

Yet one sits in the airplane and smiles over

Their release from hopeless hustle

We Came Through the Broken Door

We came through the broken door

We did not have the key

We were prepared to break the door

We had cups and swords

We were armed, not like robbers

That come with guns and swords

We were singing and clapping

I remember I almost lost my voice

We had one follower

Who led us to the door

We crossed the busy streets

Our thoughts went to those sleeping

For good or for bad

To those working night shifts

To the drunk drivers

And to the officers parading

The rioting streets

In our minds

We had to break the door

Peacefully or forcefully

Someone in there needed

Us desperately

We had to save a soul

Stains

I see the childless lady
Holding out her arms
Like one does in time
To receive the Holy Eucharist

Her hands are sweaty
Blood-stained, tears mixed with blood
She is shaky as if being struck by hunger
For days
She better open her mouth
To receive it, else she be rejected
Not different
Blistered, swollen lips
Mouth swollen with spittle
Mouth left unajar
I bet the spittle could make a cupful
Deep within, she better wash her hands
She better empty her spittle
Her hands dry and stainless, her mouth empty, unsored
Before coming to stand with us

I Lost My Virginity

I lost my virginity—
my treasure.
Overcame all temptations,
overcame my libido.
I recall living like an outcast in my home
mocked by acquaintances, well-wishers,
spies, and enemies because I chose to
preserve my virginity.
I wore a mask, yet that thief unveiled me.
Like trees cut down without reforestation
I was slowly maneuvered and destroyed by you.
Should I call this a rape?
You coerced me with your language
that I left mine for,
and now all I speak is you.
Give back my virginity.

Untitled

A friend says when I consummate

I felt nervous, I was delicate

We had it without protection

Though warned several times to take precaution

I got undressed by him

He put on a love song for me

I shook my head in declination

Even though he saw this as a celebration

The tune I detest to listen

Knowing underneath he had a truncheon

He pushed me on the couch without caution

I thought it was mere infatuation

"Don't scream too hard," he said

I shook in approval for his instruction

Experiencing Serenity

To experience serenity close your eyes tight

So tight that it hurts

So tight that you see a dark spot

A yellow, bright star in the middle

Shines and you wonder what it is

Open your eyes and look at that flashing light at your side

Turn to your side and give honor to

The one who brought you the light

Tired

Tired of thinking

Tired of reflecting

Tired of writing

Tired of reading

Tired of searching

Tired of laughing

Tired of crying

Tired of cooking

Tired of relaxing

Tired, tired, tired of worrying

Even tired of growing

Tired, tired…I cry.

The Lady

The lady moving behind you

Is your backbone

She brought good tidings to your household

She does not know the road well

You move faster than she can

She complains of the slippery, snowy path

And misses sliding several times

You move as if alone

When you turn to help

All you see are footsteps to the snowy trench

And you are alone again

Untitled

Remember long ago in the teens

I decided to undergo the journey

'Twas meant to cleanse my impurities

Reflecting past atrocities with little talk

But with my creator enriching my dumb mind with His word

A journey perfect now for many imperfections

On my path I strive to persist

Till I retreat

Winter

Nobody welcomes you

Everyone sighs at your approach

Your coming warrants a heavy pocket

We have been refreshed for a couple of months now

We are worried about cracked lips,

Pale faces, and

Persistent cough (cracking)

All complain of money missing from their pockets

In their efforts to wipe their misery away

Forgive Me

Forgive me if
I failed to satisfy you;
I failed to be a woman;
I failed to show concern;
I failed to cook for you;
I failed to make up our bed;
I failed to deep clean.
I am only human.
So, forgive me.

A Memorable Sunday

A populated one at church

As I stand on the sidewalk from beginning to end

And on a festive day

When man forgets mere courtesy and runs outside and laughs
  greatly

When parishioners mumble and grumble as the sermon halts and
  then continues

At the deeds inside

When at the altar for a song one faints and is rushed outside

And the church is noisy and with eyes wandering.

When a parishioner pumps up a hit like a bomb landing on
  concrete

When singers get stuck in a line of parishioners like a stammer
  waiting for words to pop in the head

When I have to rush outside and redirect the noisy parishioners

Who giggle about what is inside

Infants yell and the church half empty

A boring Sunday and the sermon must go on

Untitled

Treading barefoot on the unending road
The gutters of piss and orange and mango peelings
Smell of stale fish in the hot sun
And running water in my armpits
Like that from a dripping tap

I watch the posters in buildings
And hit doors asking for vacancies
And none. Persons passing with slips, bags, and checks in hands
Still I move in high expectation

When there is a smile on my face
As I ascend the stairs to the fancy name
And building and am ushered in
To the office. A long-neck dude
From the bathroom with wet hands
Stretching for a salute
Says sit down

When my tattered awards file gets flipped and approved
And when the crooked hand and huge fingers begin to
Pull my hands to proximity and danger is near
It frustrates when there is no outlet
And in my bag a bottled water
To hit underneath and rush to the outside
For another try

Whiplash

Though awful your name sounds
You nurtured and disciplined me
When I felt lazy to do my homework you reminded me with a whip
Just as when I got a bad grade am motivated to work harder
These years you are a taboo
Abusers, addicts, mentally abused kids, and wives with whiplash
The husband without notice of food at dinner kicks and lashes
    the wife and children
Tell me if you prefer being locked without food for twenty-four
    hours for disrespect and laziness
Or being given ten strokes that last merely ten minutes' pain
Whip is what formed us
It is not unfamiliar to most that forget the label on it in the foreign
    land
One gets redirection. For a child who cries without reason?
Redirect?
Child upbringing—a nightmare for parents scared of using whips
    on heady offspring
The misuse of power among humanity
Is as misuse of whips to discipline
To some, it is revenge, fun, a method to lure the woman to bed
Most will agree to be slapped, multiple kicks and whips in the
    middle of an orgasm, and never consider it abuse
Is it the pleasure or the sweet, bitter pain that makes past

memories fade?

The worried neighbor rushes and hits the door in an effort to save the abused

Hears provocative and tempting moans—compelling to report?

We allow our emotions, urges, to be satisfied and submit to subjects of whips

Is it the fear of people reporting that will be labelled abuse or the untold motive of mankind?

The Power of the Mind

The mind is like a house, harboring lots of thoughts—
Good, evil, confusion, opinions.
He is a house with lots of things.
Imagine man without that great harbor—
Stressless, useless, thoughtless, and funny.
I'm proud of my mind, which harbors
Ideas that move and inspire.
Think of a world without "minds."
There is a mind in everyone—
The mad, the crazy, the intelligent, the prostitute,
The thief, the rapist, the clergy....
The mind is crowded with lots of ideas—
Endless ideas. Can't think straight.
Where do I start? Where do I end?
I'm happy I have this great house.

Perfection

I opened all dictionaries, searched all libraries,
Ransacked all to get the definition of perfect.
Visited elements of nature—
The meadow, snow, grass, trees—in fact, everything.
Could not see or read perfection.
Looking at the grass, I found a grassless spot.
I saw a bent tree almost ready to die,
Snow spots taking different shapes.
Our lives and characters take different shapes
As the snow bends like the tree.

Knock Hard

Knock hard

For the door is closed and hard to open

They are inside

There is silence

Even the fire of a gunshot is silent

In doubt, use your fists and feet and kick hard

That steals the memory of a vacation to the Bahamas

And draws attention to the noise outside

Continue kicking and hitting

For actions make more sense than words

Avarice

Avarice

Lays his hands on everything

Never tired of amassing wealth

Overflown bank account

A yard of Mercedes Benzes, Pradas, and limos

The night encompasses pleasantries

Full of rapid eye movement

Waking fatigued to his glory

And broadened face to his stuff

Armor

Armor

Your voice like an embellished armor

That strikes the heart and leaves petals

Your slender arms fit around

My waist like an abdominal binder

Your straight, slim legs lift the saddest of souls

Your sincere smile puts me at peace

Sweet Mosquito

Tiny harmless thing

Sleeping on neighbors' windows

Singing in pairs sweet, slow jams

Behind Paul McCartney's Beatles

Come and sing in my ear the melody

Put me to sleep, sweet mosquito

And never a slap for your annoying voice

Untitled

A vaporizing house

Evoking hot, hot lava on roofs

Staining the harsh mountains

Spreading its vapor and fumes on streets

A mob outside of children, adults, and old

Lifting tearful eyes at the vapor reaching the skies

Fire extinguishers fighting each other making no sense

Dropping roofs, broken stones, broken trunks

Flying up and resting down

Souls leaping with sorrow and thoughts

Arresting minds longing for true answers

Buried deep, deep, deep down in the cruel soul

Untitled

Lost in the bush among the leaves of

Plants and flowers in the middle of spring

Inspired by the giant leaf of this great plant

The desire to plug it home

My mind telling me this would

Remedy my persistent headache if

At my bedside

I eventually plug it

Place it in my dominant hand

Scared of twisting the edges or

Risking it against the gentle wind

I place in my purse

Walking home towards the

Tail of the forest, I get robbed and lose my purse

Crying, I run to the bush and find a leafless plant

I leave for home

Think of Myself

Think of myself
Think of myself shedding in my dreams
Think of myself
Think of myself pouring out in my dreams
Think of myself
Think of myself weeping in my dreams
Think of myself
Think of myself wet in my dreams
Wet face, wet neck, wet trunk
Radiating to my back
Wetness in me, wetness in my hips, legs, and feet
So warm and hot
So comfortable to open my eyes and to open my dreams
To realize I had a dream

We are getting old
When we speak to our makeup instead of makeup to us
We are getting old when our faces look and feel
Different from other body parts
When our necks are decorated with veins and neck as duck
We are getting old when the comb steals pieces of hair with each
    application
When we can count hair pieces in winter
We are even getting old when we can't speak fast
And have difficulty comprehending the process
And still growing in the process

CPSIA information can be obtained
at www.ICGtesting.com
Printed in the USA
BVOW04s2053110517
483459BV00024B/46/P